Happiness Through Life Organization

Organize Your Home, Plan Your Future, Achieve Your Goals and Attain Happiness

Table of Contents

Introduction

This book contains proven steps and strategies on how to achieve happiness by organizing all the important aspects of your life.

Most people have developed bad habits over time that eventually lead to a disorganized life. When you suffer from a disorganized life, your life becomes more stressful and toxic, and you start feeling unhappy. A disorganized life can also have negative effects on your mental health. In fact, a disorganized life may be a symptom of something serious like depression or an anxiety disorder. You may also be depriving yourself of happiness and success by allowing disorder to take over. A cluttered life affects how other people perceive you, how well you perform at work, and even the way you eat.

This book will help you create a happier and more fulfilling life by organizing all of life's important components. You can use this book to help organize your home and workspace, identify your goals, and manage your tasks. This book can also help you organize your financial life and create more fulfilling relationships. Take control of your life with the helpful and easy to use tips right here in this book.

Chapter 1 - Why Is It Important To Organize Your Home And Your Life?

Success and happiness do not just happen. They are products of hard work and conscious effort. According to many psychologists and mental health experts, happiness is a choice, and there are many ways to be happy. You can eliminate negative emotions such as jealousy, anger, pessimism and resentment, in addition to cultivating positive emotions like gratitude, serenity, compassion and empathy.

However, to achieve happiness, optimum productivity and success, you also need to organize your life. One of the most important keys to happiness, success and consistency is to keep yourself organized. This principle applies to every aspect of your life from your home to your goals, your activities to your time, and your relationships to your finances.

When you become organized, it is easier for you to plan ahead and set goals. An organized life is a life that has a clear direction. When you organize the many aspects of your life, it becomes easier to achieve your dreams and goals. In turn, you will feel happier and more fulfilled.

When you organize your home and your life, you are more likely to achieve your dreams. You will also have an easier time managing your time. If your house is a mess, finding the most mundane objects, like your car keys, can turn into a time-wasting ordeal. When you are organized, you have more time for the people you love and the activities that are important to you.

Staying organized will make your life easier and the easier your life is, the happier you will be. If your life is not organized, then you are struggling to get by. You simply float through life. When you organize your life, you gain the ability to surpass your potential and live the life you always dreamed of.

Chapter 2 - Principles For Organizing Your Home

Many psychologists agree there is a correlation between happiness and a well organized, clean home. In fact, studies show that children who grew up in clean and well-organized homes have more financial and academic success than those who grew up in messy, disorganized homes.

When your home is neatly organized, you can have peace of mind. It becomes easier to move around, and you can save a lot of time. You also become more relaxed and comfortable in your own home. Looking at a messy space day after day has a negative effect on your mood and your outlook. You are more likely to feel down and depressed if your house is full of clutter and messes.

Here are some of the many benefits to maintaining a clean and well-organized home:

- ✦ Sanitation – When you clean and organize your home, you remove dust and bacteria that can cause allergies and diseases. This reduces the risk of contracting diseases caused by dust and germs.

- ✦ Improves mood – As mentioned earlier, you experience better moods if your house is clean and neat.

- ✦ Lowers the risk of injury – When your home is full of clutter, the people living in it are prone to different kinds of injuries. Toys and other items on the floor increase the risk of trips and falls.

⊥ Reduces stress - When your house is neat and tidy, you are just about halfway to a stress-free life. You stress less about missing items and what your friends might think of the mess.

Organizing your home is easier than you think. In fact, once you have organized your home, it is relatively easy to maintain it. Here are some important tips to use in keeping your home simple, neat and well organized:

1. Schedule a declutter day – It would take you a long time to organize your home the way it is now, so it is important to schedule a declutter day. You can do this on your day off from work. If you want a tidy home, then you have to invest time and effort in making that happen. Once you are done, it will all have been worth it.

2. Invest in clear boxes and label – If you have a small living space, then it would be wise to invest in clear storage boxes and stickers. You can write on stickers to label the boxes and drawers. This makes it easier for you to find items you need.

3. Keep your front entrance and lawn clean – Your lawn is where it all starts. Try your best to keep it neat, well lit, and clutter-free. Make it a habit to mow your lawn regularly. Feng Shui experts believe that your front entrance is central to your home, so keeping it clean is crucial.

4. Let the energy flow freely in and out of your home – The universe is filled with energy. If you want to live a peaceful and happy life,

then you have to let the energy flow freely through your home. This promotes harmony, relaxation, and health. Clutter and awkwardly placed furniture blocks this energy, so it is important to put some thought into the furniture arrangement.

5. Get rid of the things you no longer use – Most of us like to keep things we no longer use for various reasons, but to keep your life simple, you have to get rid of what you do not need anymore. You can sell, donate, or give away any useful items. Otherwise, they likely belong in the garbage. Remember, the less stuff you have, the better. When you adopt a minimalist perspective like this, you save a lot of space, time and money.

6. Leave room for "future" stuff – You will definitely accumulate more belongings in the future, so be sure to leave room for those eventual purchases.

7. Do not buy stuff just because it is on sale – Many people end up buying things they do not need because of a sale. This is a waste of money and space, so before buying items for the house, ask yourself if you are really going to use it. If not, do not buy it.

8. Keep the things you use frequently accessible – Identify what you use frequently and make sure it is accessible. Do not store these items away. Make sure they are visible and can be located easily.

9. Clean and organize one room at a time – Cleaning and organizing your home can be an

overwhelming task. To make it easier, you have to clean and organize one room at a time. We will discuss how to clean and organize each room in your house in the following chapters. If you live with your family, then you can assign one person to clean a specific room to make organizing easier.

Remember, when you organize your home, you are setting yourself up for success. You are on your way to living a happy and stress-free life.

Chapter 3 - How To Organize Your Bedroom

Your bedroom is your personal space. If you want to be truly happy and at peace, then you have to organize and declutter your bedroom. Waking up in a cluttered bedroom is not a good way to start your day. A cluttered bedroom can immediately drain your energy upon waking.

On the other hand, looking at a clean and organized bedroom is the ideal way to wake up. It creates instant peace of mind and positive vibes. When your space is organized, you feel relaxed, energized, and ready to start the day. You do not have to spend time picking up scattered items or cleaning your room after you wake up in the morning. This allows you to focus on more important things.

Here are some of the steps you can take to declutter your bedroom:

1. Get two boxes and sort everything. Label the first box "must go" and label the second box "keep." Go through everything in your room and identify what you want to keep and what needs to go. Put the things you want to keep inside the second box and put the things you want to donate or throw away in the first box.

   After you have identified what you want to keep and what you want to let go, you must go through the two boxes again.

   Go through the "keep" box and determine what stays in your room and what goes into a cabinet or storage box for future use. After this, go through the "must go" box. Identify what will be donated and thrown away.

2. Take everything off of your bed. Remove your cell phone, dirty clothes, or other things lying on your bed. Clean the mattress and wash the beddings. Place new bedding on the mattress and spray some cologne or perfume on the bedding to make it smell great. Creating an inviting bed makes a huge difference in your bedroom.

   Neatly arrange the pillows and stuffed animals, if any, on your bed. Remove everything from under your bed and find a new home for it. According to Feng Shui expert, you will be unlucky in love and career if you store anything under your bed.

3. Take out the furniture items you do not need. Do you have too many dressers or chairs in your bedroom that you do not use? Think of what you can give away, sell, or donate. You can also move the furniture items you do not need to a different room.

4. Organize your nightstand or bedside table. Take everything out and off of your nightstand. Clean it thoroughly. Go through the items you removed from your nightstand, and choose what you want to keep and what you want to throw or give away. Throw away empty containers and expired vitamins and medicines.

   Protect your nightstand by using felt pads. This prevents scratches. You can buy felt pads at the store or you can buy felt paper from the craft store and cut it to match the shape of your lampshade or phone.

If you have a lampshade, clean it and put it on top of your nightstand. You can also put your desktop calendar, phone, and alarm clock on it. Put the important items such as cell phone, wallet, and car keys in the top drawer of the dresser. Place items like your lotion, night cream, eye cream, pens, and eye pads inside the second drawer. You can also place a bottle of water in the second drawer. It is best to keep water in your room in case you get thirsty in the middle of the night. This way, you do not have to go to the kitchen to get water late at night.

5. Many people read in their rooms. If you have a bookshelf in your room, you need to organize it, as well. Remove all the books from the shelf and clean it thoroughly. Sort out your books before putting them back in the shelf.

   If you are a student, sort your books according to subjects. However, if you just read for pleasure, sort your books by genre – horror, romance, self-help, recipe books, and instructional books. You can also sort your books by author. If you have a large bookshelf and you watch television in your room, you can also place your DVDs on your bookshelf. Sort your DVDs by title or by genre.

6. If you keep your shoes in your room, organize them too. If you do not have a shoe rack or cabinet, then invest in one. Remember to keep your shoes in an open space. Otherwise, the shoes may develop a foul odor.

When organizing your shoes, sort them by use. Place your work shoes on the top shelf, your sandals on the second shelf, and your running shoes on the third shelf.

Here are some amazing shoe-storage ideas to help you save space:

- Use special hangers for shoes on your wall to produce a beautiful shoe display.

- Store your shoes inside an ottoman. The ottoman works as a chair and as storage. When you do this, you save space.

- Use a repurposed ladder to hang your stilettos on.

- Use a shoe organizer, and hang it on your wall or the back of your door.

- Place the shoes in a large basket.

7. If you have limited clothing space, then you need to be smart in organizing your clothes. The first thing to do is take out all of your clothes from the closet. Again, identify the clothes you are going to keep and the clothes you are going to donate, sell, or throw away. Here are some tips that you can use in organizing your clothes:

- Buy tags you can write on – If you are serious about organizing your clothes, invest in tags. You can use these tags on boxes, hangers, and storage bags.

- Organize your clothes by days – If you want to have a stress-free morning, try planning your outfits a week ahead. This will save you time. Planning your outfit ahead also ensures you look good. Use writable tags to write the days of the week.

+ Organize the rest of your clothes by color – Try organizing the clothes you are not going to use for the week by color. Fold pants and place them on one shelf, and hang up shirts, blouses, dresses, and blazers.

+ Use photo frames to organize your dangling earrings – You can use old photo frames to organize these normally chaotic pieces of jewelry. Put glue on a corkboard in the frame and hang your earrings from the foam.

+ Use belt hangers – You can buy belt hangers from the department store. One hanger can hold four to six belts. Using belt hangers helps keep your closet neat and organized. It saves space, too.

+ Place your stud earrings inside pill holders – Pill boxes can also double as stud earrings safe boxes. Place one pair each box.

+ Use a towel rack to create a jewelry rack – You can use hooks to hang your necklaces on a towel rack to avoid tangling them in a jewelry box. The jewelry rack is also a great way to add elegance and sophistication to your room.

+ Tie your neckties and scarves on a hanger – You can tie up to four scarves or neckties on one hanger. This saves space and helps you find your neckties and scarves faster.

+ Keep all your towels in one drawer – Also, consider sorting them by color.

+ Keep your bed sheets and pillowcases in one drawer – Store the matching bed sheets and pillowcases together to make it easier to find them.

+ Buy a lingerie and underwear organizer – Place the lingerie organizer inside your closet drawer and sort your underwear by color.

+ Put all your bags in an ottoman – An ottoman is the best place to store all your bags and purses, if you wish to optimize space. You can also install hooks on your wall and hang your bags on them.

8. Clean your bedroom windows and replace your curtains. If you want to keep your room dust-free, you have to clean your windows and replace your curtains often. When buying curtains, choose some that fit the motif and color of your room.

Your bedroom is your sanctuary. It reflects your mood, your disposition and your state of mind. If you want happiness, peace of mind, and success, you have to ensure your room reflects that. When your bedroom is clean and organized, you instantly feel more at peace and happy. Plus, it is always great to wake up to a clean and organized room.

Chapter 4 - How To Organize Your Kitchen

The kitchen is one of the most important rooms in your house. This is where you prepare and cook your food. Some people entertain their guests in their kitchen too.

Your kitchen is the heart of your home where a lot of money is usually invested in appliances, fixtures, and furniture. Thus, if you want to maintain a happy and stress-free life, you have to organize and clean your kitchen.

Here are the steps to cleaning and organizing your kitchen:

1. Remove everything from your kitchen cabinets – To clean and organize your kitchen effectively, you have to remove everything from your cabinets. Donate or throw away what you do not need anymore, like empty bottles. Also, eliminate duplicate items. Remember, the simpler your home is, the happier you will become.

2. Sort your items – For a simple and stress-free life, you have to group similar items. Arrange all your baking and cooking items together, place all the utensils in one drawer, and group all your glasses and plates together.

3. Use clear storage containers – To properly organize your kitchen and maximize your kitchen space, it is best to use containers to store your kitchen and cooking items. Group

together items like gravy mixes, cereals, and sauce mixes.

4. Use Drawer Organizers – Drawer organizers and dividers are ideal for storing utensils. If you use drawer dividers, then it becomes easier to find things.

5. Label Boxes – It is often hard to find things in the kitchen, and it can be frustrating to waste time looking for the bread knife or can opener. If you want your life to be simpler, then it is best to put a label on your drawers and boxes. This way, you do not have to spend so much time looking for things. Instead, you can spend that time on more important things in your life.

6. Clean your Refrigerator – You store many food items in your refrigerator, so it is important to keep it clean and organized. Remove all the items from your refrigerator and throw away expired and stale food. Clean your fridge thoroughly and neatly arrange all the food. Remember to clean and organize your refrigerator at least once a week. This only takes a few minutes of your time, but cleaning your refrigerator yields many benefits.

When you declutter your kitchen, it becomes easier to move around, cook your favorite foods, and find what you need. You will be more productive and have time to do more important things.

Chapter 5 - How To Organize The Living Room?

The living room is the first thing you see when you enter your home, so it is important to keep it clean and organized. Your living room can actually have many functions, including a place for your family to relax and an area to entertain friends. Whatever you use your living room for, it is essential to keep it neat. When you have a clean living room, you feel happier and more relaxed.

Here are some tips for organizing and cleaning your living room:

1. Identify all the activities that usually happen in your living room. Do you use your living room to watch TV, do aerobic exercise, entertain guests, read, or play?

2. Divide the room into different zones. Each zone should cater to one activity. You can place the TV in one zone and the piano in another. However, sometimes different zones and functions overlap, which is okay.

3. Keep your living room clutter free – Pick up the books and toys off the floor. Arrange the small decorative figurines inside a glass cabinet if you have one. You can also place them on top of your coffee table.

4. Hang photo frames on the wall – To save space, it is best to hang photos on the wall instead of setting them out. Photos have great

decorative value, bring back many happy memories, and create good vibes.

5. Simplify – If you want a happy life, you need to simplify your home, including your living room. Get rid of the items you no longer use. You can throw them away, recycle them, give them away, or donate them. Also, resist buying too many decorative items. This will save you money and make your living room look more neat and organized.

Your living room mirrors your personality and affects your outlook, so you should keep it tidy and orderly. If you want to live a happier life, then you also have to keep it simple. Do not buy unnecessary and expensive items for your living room. Your future self will thank you for it.

Chapter 6 - Set Goals

If you want to organize and sort out your life, you must set goals. Goals give your life direction and encourage you to use your resources wisely. You also use your time more effectively, make better decisions and achieve peace of mind. When you have goals, it is easier to achieve what you really want in life and make forward progress. Goal setting increases the chances of achieving prosperity, improves your self-confidence, and motivates you to take control of your life. It also increases hope and optimism and brings a sense of control to your life.

To have full control over your life, start by setting goals. Goals give you a strong sense of purpose and direction. If you are not sure how to set goals, then here are some tips to get you started:

1. Choose goals to jumpstart a journey

Before you set your goals, you have to ask yourself the following questions:

- What makes me happy?

- What do I want to do for the rest of my life?

- Who do I want to spend time with and collaborate with?

- What do I really want?

To set the right goals, you have to identify your values and principles. Identify the things that are important to you. You should formulate your goals based on your deepest desires, values and principles because this keeps you motivated. When your goal is important to you, you do your best to achieve it.

2. Your goals should be SMART

To achieve your goals, they have to be SMART (Specific, Measurable, Attainable, Relevant, and Time bound). SMART goals are powerful, and they are easier to achieve.

- Specific – Your goal must be well defined, clear and specific. Generalized goals are vague and do not have a strong force. Remember that goals give you a sense of direction, and the direction should be clear, specific, and precise.

- Measurable – You should be able to measure your goal. Include amounts and any kind of numerical value to your goal to make it easier to track your success and progress. Do not make one of your goals "to save." This goal has no force. Instead, specify how much you want to save by a specific deadline.

- Achievable – Your goal should be attainable. If you set a goal that is almost impossible to achieve, you are setting yourself up for failure. You should set realistic goals. However, do not fall into the trap of setting goals that are too easy to achieve. If you do this, you will not experience a significant change in your life.

- Relevant – Your goals have to be relevant to your life and career. They must align with your principles and values and be important to you.

* Time-bound – For your goals to be powerful, you have to set a deadline. When you do not have a deadline, you will not act in sufficient time. A deadline creates a strong sense of urgency to act right away.

3. Put your goals into writing – When you write down your goals, it is easier for you to achieve them. Written goals are more powerful and forceful, and when you write your goals, use "will" instead of "may" or "might." For example, write something like, "I will lose 20 pounds in 2 months."

4. Prioritize goals – After you have written all your goals, it is important to prioritize them. Not all goals are equal. Some are more important than the others, and you must decide which one is the most important. Rate your goals according to their importance and how you plan to achieve them.

5. Start working on goal #1 – After prioritizing your goals, start working toward your first goal. To do this, eliminate all your self-limiting beliefs and start believing in yourself unconditionally. Be proactive and take the necessary action to achieve your goals.

Chapter 7 - Formulate Action Plans

In order to achieve your goals, you have to formulate action plans for each goal. An action plan is an intricate and detailed plan that outlines the actions needed to reach a specific goal.

An action plan requires dedicated time and thought. You also have to allot time to test your plan to see if it is effective. Create a flow chart or sub-goals below your main goal.

For example, if your goal is to lose 20 pounds in one month, here is a sample action plan:

Goal: Lost 20 Pounds in One Month				
Action Items	Day 1	Day 2	Day 3	Day 4
Work out for 2 hours daily ⬇ Walk and Jog for 1 Hour ⬇ Do Aerobics exercise for another 1 hour				
Limit carbohydrate and fat intake ⬇ Eliminate rice and white bread from the diet ⬇ Do not eat cake and cookies ⬇ Do not drink soda and				

sugary juices				
Eat more fruits and Vegetables ↓ Eat vegetables and fruits every meal				

Drink at least 8 glasses of water a day
 	
   ↓ Drink 2 glasses of water after waking up
 	
   ↓ Drink one glass of water before every meal
 	
   ↓ Drink one glass of water after every meal
 	
   ↓ Drink one glass of water before sleeping				

Monitor weight daily				

Track your progress and monitor your adherence to the action plan. Once you have formulated an action plan, place small checklists under each sub-goal to monitor your progress

It is also important to reward yourself for following your action plan. When you reward yourself, it becomes easier to follow through in the future. Here are some of the ways you can reward yourself for following your action plans or reaching a milestone:

   ↓ Take a relaxing bubble bath

   ↓ Watch your favorite soap opera or TV series

- Take a nap

- Buy yourself an ice cream

- Treat yourself to the spa

- Get a manicure or pedicure

- Get a haircut

- Buy new clothes

- Go to a party

- Get a massage

- Go shopping

- Go to the beach

You can give yourself big or small rewards based on the accomplishment.

When you have an action plan to follow, reaching your goals and achieving your dreams becomes easier than ever. Having clear and detailed sub-goals can also make it easier to reach your goals. You stay focused and organized, and as a result, your life will fill with happiness and purpose.

Chapter 8 - Fighting Procrastination

If you want to live a happy and organized life, then you have to eliminate procrastination. Upon eliminating procrastination, you become more productive and accomplish more in the time you have. Procrastination is simply a product of poor organization. Therefore, if you want to stop procrastinating and start living a happier life, you have to get organized.

Here are the ways to prevent procrastination through organization:

1. Audit your time

Most of us go through life without knowing where our time went. If you want to be happy and live a productive life, then you should follow where your time is going. Understanding how you spend your days, weeks, months and years can help you make the best of your time.

You have to account both your free time and work time. Scheduling both your work time and free time creates a smart format to keep you productive.

2. Prioritize

Most people procrastinate because they do not know where to start, and they feel overwhelmed by all the tasks they have to do. If you want to fight procrastination and live a productive life, you have to prioritize the most important tasks.

It is best to prioritize one task daily. Before you start your day, determine which task is the most important and finish it first.

3. Eliminate Distractions

We live in the age of Facebook, Twitter, and other social networking sites, so it is easy to get distracted. If you want to stay organized and fight procrastination, then you have to commit to removing distractions. Resist the urge to check Facebook, Twitter, and gossip sites. When you need to finish something important, also turn off your phone or at least put it on silent mode.

4. Divide a large project into small tasks

As mentioned earlier, people procrastinate because they get overwhelmed with a huge project or task. In order to eliminate procrastination, try breaking down a large project into reasonably small tasks. This way, you feel less overwhelmed and more organized.

5. Organize your workspace

In order to eliminate procrastination, you have to organize your workspace. When your workspace is neat and well organized, it is easier for you to move about. You will also find it easier to focus. This is a topic in a following chapter.

6. Eliminate perfectionism

Perfectionism is one of the most common causes of procrastination. Many people put off tasks they think they cannot do perfectly. If you want to fight procrastination, then you must accept that perfect is not necessary as long as you do your best. High standards are fine, but it is not wise to set impossible standards. Your best is enough.

7. List all the things you have been putting off

To fight procrastination and get your life back on track, you have to start doing the things you have been putting off. To do this, list everything you have put off and incorporate each item into your daily "to do" list.

8. Give up your excuses

Procrastinators are great at making excuses. If you want to live a happy life, then you have to take care of your responsibilities. Give up your excuses and start thinking about the benefits of accomplishing the task.

9. Just do it

Nike's slogan says it all. Just do it. Do not wait for tomorrow, for the economy to be better, or for gay marriage to be legalized in all states in America. You have to just do it.

When you fight procrastination, your life start moving forward. You will live a productive and more fulfilling life. If you eliminate procrastination, you will be happier and less stressed because you do not have to rush to beat your deadlines anymore.

Chapter 9 - How To Organize Your Work Space

Whether you work in a corporate office or the comfort of your home, it is necessary to have a clean, well-organized workspace.

Clearing your workspace yields many benefits such as increasing your work efficiency. Most people spend too much time on minor things like looking for a file or a pen. If you organize your desk, your email, and your files, it is easier to get things done. As a result, you can complete more work in a day.

Clearing your workspace also reduces stress. Having a messy and cluttered desk can be very stressful. You are more likely to feel pressured and frustrated if you cannot locate a file urgently needed for a meeting or client presentation.

A neat and tidy workplace also enhances your professional image. According to a survey, human resource managers said that the appearance of an employee's workspace greatly affects their opinion and perception of that employee's level of professionalism.

When you have a clean workspace, it gives you a strong sense of accomplishment. Having a clean workspace also makes you feel good.

Here are some tips you can use in cleaning and organizing your workspace:

1. Get rid of things you do not want or need – The simpler your office space, the better. To declutter and tidy up your workspace, you

have to eliminate the things you do not want or need. Go through all your possessions and determine what you need for work and what you can do without. Throw away or give away the things you do not need.

2. Create a physical inbox – Many companies do paperless transactions most of the time, and because of this, most desks do not have a physical inbox anymore. If you want to organize your workspace, then you need to have a physical inbox on your desk to sort all mail and papers into.

3. Place a trashcan near your desk. If you want to have an organized workspace, then you have to place a trashcan within reach of your desk to encourage you to throw out any garbage right away.

4. Clear out the paper clutter by scanning it – One simple way to eliminate clutter in your office is to scan all the papers and keep a soft copy instead. If you need a paper copy later on, you can just print the scanned version.

5. Label everything – If you want to find your materials easily, it will help to label everything. You can label your desk drawer, the boxes, and the folders. This can also help other people find things in case you are out of the office.

6. Organize your desktop – Keep your computer and phone clean. You can use office organizers to keep your desktop clean and organized like the trays for papers, pens, staplers, and markers. Keep only your office essentials on your desktop.

7. Use storage boxes or filing cabinets – Use filing cabinets or storage boxes to store your archived files. Remember that you only need to keep the files you might need later on. If you know you will not need the files again, then do not keep them.

8. Organize your work-related files – Organize your computer files in folders. This way, it is easier = to find files. It is also necessary to back up your files in case your computer crashes. You can use a thumb drive or online file storage like Google drive or Dropbox.

9. Sort your email – To sort your email, you need to organize by sender. Read the emails sent by your boss first as they may be important. You can also set your email to automatically send spam messages or messages from Facebook and Twitter directly to the trash. It is also helpful to create folders, so you can move the email to a specific folder first thing in the morning and read it later on when you have time.

When you organize your workspace, you will feel more relaxed and focused on the important things. Since you become productive, you will be happier and more successful in life.

Chapter 10 - Making An Effective To Do List

To effectively organize your day, you have to make a "To Do" list. A to do list creates order and enables you to manage your tasks and time on a daily basis. It also allows you to prioritize tasks, establish accountability, and decide what to delegate.

Here are some helpful tips you can use in writing your "To Do" list:

1. Write your "To Do" list the night before.

You have to dedicate a few minutes of your day to think about the things you need to do and accomplish. When you put thought into your to do list, you will not miss out anything.

2. Qualify the contents of your "To Do" list.

It is important to qualify the contents of your "To Do" list. List things that are important and that you must do. If you can delegate the task, then use your to do list to determine that.

3. Assign Estimated Time

To effectively organize your day and your time, assign time estimates to you "To Do" items.

4. Do not confuse quality with quantity

If you have many items on your "to do" list, you are not necessarily being productive. Again, you have to make sure that the items on your "to do" list match your goals. If your goal is to become a successful entrepreneur, then it is important to create daily tasks to help you achieve your goal. Keep your "to do" list simple. Many life coaches recommend you only put three non-negotiable tasks on your daily "to do" list. You can do the rest of the items on the list only after you are done with the three non-negotiable items.

5. Make time for your leisure activities

In order to live a happy and balanced life, it is important to make time for leisure activities. Incorporate fun activities into your daily schedule to keep you grounded and reduce the stress brought on by work.

You can write your to do list in your paper planner or in an electronic planner. Cross off items on your list and give yourself a small reward as you complete them.

A "to do" list keeps you on track. This list is an important component in giving your life a sense of purpose and in helping you become more organized.

Chapter 11 - Organize Your Finances

It is true that money cannot buy happiness, but a disorganized financial life can certainly cause problems and unhappiness. If you want to live a simple, organized, and happy life, you have to sort out your finances.

When you organize your finances, you have a strong control over your money. A budget is one way to be seriously intentional about how and where you spend your money. When you organize your finances, you take control of your money, so it does not control you. Organizing your finances also helps you work on your money goals. When you budget your money and organize your financial life, you avoid spending too much on services and items that are not aligned with your financial goals. Organizing your financial life ensures a bright future.

Here are some tips to help you organize your financial life and live a happier and more stress-free life:

1. Prepare a monthly budget.

To ensure you reach your financial goals, you have to prepare a monthly budget. You have to spend a few minutes of your time to ensure you have a feasible and effective monthly budget. Here is how you can prepare your budget.

➕ Track your monthly income - Do you have a fixed salary? Are you an entrepreneur who has an erratic monthly income? To make a feasible monthly budget, you have to determine the amount you take home every month. Deduct taxes and other costs from your salary to determine your net income.

+ Determine your expenditures – List all your essential monthly expenses like the mortgage, health expenses, food, utility bills, car payments, and gas. Break down your expenditures into different categories like food, bills, travel and leisure, transportation, health and fitness, savings, shopping, etc.

+ Compare your income and expenditures – Are your expenses larger than your income? If they are, you are in big trouble because it means you are not living within your means.

+ Create financial goals – Do you want to save money? How much do you want to have saved? Do you want to be debt-free in a year? Do you want to save for your retirement? Do you want to save for a business venture or do you want to have enough money to travel around the world? When you have financial goals, your financial life becomes more organized.

+ Pay yourself first – You need to incorporate savings into your monthly budget. Ideally, your savings should be around 20 to 30 percent of your monthly income, but 10 percent is actually enough. Before you spend anything, make sure to pay yourself first. Do not spend the money allotted for savings.

+ Make a list of the essential expenses – List all the things you must consume or pay for like credit card bills, car loans, mortgage, food, utility bills, cell phone bills, and others.

+ Make a budget for discretionary items – This is where you determine how much money you plan to spend for shopping, new gadgets, travel, or fine dining. Your discretionary items say a lot about you and your values like what kind of person you are and what things are important to you. Some people prefer material items over a vacation and vice versa.

+ Use software – There is plenty of software available to help you budget your expenses. You can use BudgetPulse, Mint, Microsoft Money, Quicken, or AceMoney. Choose the software that works for you.

2. Track your expenses – After you have determined your budget, track your expenses on a daily basis. This ensures you are on the right track. Most budgeting software allows you to track and list your expenses on a daily basis. If you are not using a software program, you can keep an "expenses journal" where you record all of your expenses.

3. Avoid going over the budget – You should not go over your budget to ensure you are on your way to reaching your financial goals.

4. Do not bring your credit card – Cash is always king. If you want to have a stress-free financial life, you have to stick to your budget and leave

your credit card at home. Only use your credit card when it is absolutely necessary. Avoid spending money you do not have yet. Remember that your credit card payment history contributes a lot to your credit score, so it is absolutely necessary to only charge what you can afford to pay for.

5. Pay your bills via electronic funds transfer – Set an auto payment for your utility bills. This saves you time and money, and it ensures the bills are paid on time. However, it is important to review your bills, too, to make sure all the charges are correct. It will be difficult to ask for a refund for billing errors if you do not check your bills regularly.

6. Open two bank accounts – You should have at least two bank accounts. One account should be for bill payments and expenses and the other bank account should be used for savings. You must separate savings from the money you use for essential and discretionary expenses. This ensures you do not spend your savings on an expensive dinner or a night out with friends.

7. Discuss your budget with your partner – If you have a spouse or a partner, then you should create the budget together. This way, you know each other's expenditures and can create joint financial goals. This measure can also help prevent a misunderstanding down the road.

When you have an organized financial life, it is easier to reach your goals. You will live a less stressful life and have greater peace of mind.

Chapter 12 - Making Time For Relationships

Many people spend so much time making money and trying hard to be the best in their chosen career that they forget how important it is to spend time with their loved ones.

Part of living an organized and happy life is to spend time with people who matter to you. You have to plan very carefully and keep an open line of communication with your family and friends.

Here are some tips to keep in touch with family and friends and strengthen your relationship with them:

1. Reevaluate your schedule

Are you so focused on your work that you have completely forgotten to spend time with the important people in your life? Remember, your job is just a job. If you have aging parents, then you have to spend time with them. Life is temporary, and you cannot know when their time will be up. If you have been neglecting your spouse or kids, then you should spend at least a few hours of your week with them.

2. Plan for time with loved ones

As mentioned in earlier chapters, you have to incorporate time with your family into your daily schedule. A meeting may be important but quality time with your parents is important, too. You have to schedule time with family into your monthly calendar.

3. Take your parents on a date at least once a month

If you live in the same city, then you should take your folks out on a dinner, movie, or lunch date often. This would mean a lot to them. When you do this, you will have fewer regrets later on when they are gone. Before it is too late, try to find time for your folks. If your parents live in another state or another country, call them as often as you can.

4. Play with your kids

If you still have little children, it is essential to find time to play with them and spend quality time with them. When you do this, you get to know them better and they get to know you better. Studies show that spending time with your kids improves their academic performance, and it decreases the risk of drug abuse and teenage rebellion.

5. Do not miss meal times

To maintain a happy life, you have to eat meals with your family. Having meals together strengthens your bonding and gives you time to talk about each other's days and activities.

6. Travel with your loved ones at least once a year

You have been working hard, so it is time to reward yourself by scheduling a family vacation. Do this at least once a year. You can go to the beach or you can explore another state or country. Traveling is a powerful way to create a strong bond between people.

7. Schedule a coffee date or night out with your old friends

To live a happy life, you have to schedule a regular meet-up with your old friends. You can have cold bottles of beer together or a coffee together in a local coffee shop. These dates are a great way to catch up. You get to hear your friends' amazing stories and adventures and they get to hear yours. Remember that your friends will always have your back when things get tough, so it is important to keep in touch with them.

The time spent with your family and friends is certainly a time well spent. It strengthens your bond, and when you spend quality time with the people who matter to you, you will live a happier and a more meaningful life.

Chapter 13 - Celebrate Your Success And Share Best Practices To Others

Once you have successfully organized your life, it is essential to celebrate this great achievement. Here are some of the ideas for celebrating this milestone:

1. Thank all the people who have helped you organize your life and achieve your goals.

2. Eat out.

3. Go to a spa.

4. Write a blog entry about your journey to an organized life.

5. Buy yourself something nice.

6. Go on a night out with friends.

7. Read a book.

8. Buy yourself a piece of jewelry.

9. Go on a road trip.

10. Get a new haircut.

11. Enjoy a good cup of coffee and a slice of your favorite dessert.

12. Have a party.

After you have successfully organized your life and achieved your goals, it is time to share your success story with other people. You should share your best practices and help other people get organized and live a happy and successful life, too.

Becoming organized will drastically change the course of your life for the better. When you have a more organized life, you will attract more opportunities and more people to help you make things happen. When you have an organized life, you will have much less stress. Life will be simpler and happier.

Conclusion

I hope this book was able to help you organize your home and finances, manage your relationships, and achieve your goals and dreams.

The next step is to apply everything you learned from this book to live a happier and more organized life. The tips and techniques contained in this book are worthless if you do not use them to improve your life. Use the lessons you learned from this book to live a better life.

If you find the techniques and strategies contained in this book helpful, share them with other people in your life who may need them. Use this book to help you achieve a happier, more organized life and to help others achieve an organized and happy life, as well. One of the goals of this book is to help as many people as possible.

Thank you and good luck!

www.ingramcontent.com/pod-product-compliance
Lightning Source LLC
Chambersburg PA
CBHW070507290526
45790CB00003B/1129